How Did I Get Into This Mess?

You Compromised, Saith the Lord

By

Brenda Diann Johnson

W0006407

ASWIFTT PUBLISHING, LLC
Duncanville, Texas 75138
www.aswifttpublishing.com
Book Cover Design by
Brenda Diann Johnson

Copyright © 2012 Brenda Diann Johnson

All Rights Reserved

No part of this book may be reproduced, stored in a retrieval system, or transmitted by any means, electronic, mechanical, photocopying, recording, or otherwise, without written permission from the author.

Brenda Diann Johnson
brendadiannjohnson@yahoo.com

Published by
ASWIFTT PUBLISHING, LLC
P.O. Box 380669
Duncanville, Texas 75138

ISBN: 978-0-9847015-1-3

Library of Congress Control Number: 2011963204

How Did I Get Into This Mess?
You Compromised, Saith the Lord (2nd Ed. 2/2012)

Printed in the United States of America.

All scripture quotations are from the King James Version of the Bible. All definitions are from The Random House College Dictionary, Revised Ed.

Cover Design and Editing by Brenda Diann Johnson
Cover Photo © 2010 Elena Elisseeva

Dedications

Through pain, tears, tragedies, traumas, deaths, heartache, divorce and starting over, I dedicate this book to a MIGHTY GOD. He saw me through every situation that came up in my life. From the day I was born until now, he has been a father and husband to me. He knows all about me. God is the one who predestined me before I was born.

I dedicate this book to my father and mother. I want to thank you for giving me life and bringing me into this world. Thank you for caring for me as a young child. I also want to thank you for a rich maternal and paternal heritage.

I dedicate this book to my aunt Rosie Willis, who has been a co-parent throughout my life. She nurtured and took care of me as a child and as an adult. She helped me through major tragedies and turning points in my life. She is an asset to me. Thank you for helping me understand my maternal heritage.

I also dedicate this book to my spiritual mother, Mary Sterling, who I met at age 18. I am so glad I was introduced to her by my mother. I learned many things in her Sunday school class. Her teaching helped prepare me for the call on my life as a teacher. She has been an excellent mentor. She prayed for me during the tragedies that came in my life. I thank God for sending spiritual mothers and fathers to fill in the gap where our biological parents could not reach us.

I also dedicate this book to my true friends. I praise God

for those who walk with me in prosperity and adversity. Those who I share things in confidence and who will pray for me sincerely. Those who have cried and sought God for me. I am grateful for such friends who want to see me healed and ultimately conformed to Christ's image.

I dedicate this book to my daughter Diamond. She is my pride and joy. She is a gift that God gave me on Christmas day in 1996. While she was in my womb I gave her back to God and prayed over her. I prayed concerning what I should name her. God gave me the answer one early morning. Her name is Diamond because she is one of God's precious jewels. Her middle name is Lena in remembrance of my grandmother Lena Taplin-Johnson. Her last name is Starling because of her paternal heritage.

Last but not least, I dedicate this book to Kamille. She is my youngest daughter who has brought me much joy. I am proud to be her mother. She is an inspiration to me. June 4, 2003 was not only exciting but a blessing when she was born. Her middle name Esstine honors her grandmother and her last name is Padgitt because of the heritage she has from her father.

I also dedicate this book to family members and friends both saved and unsaved.

God bless you all,

Brenda Diann Johnson

Acknowledgments

Finally this book has come into existence. God put this message inside me many years ago and told me to write a book. I did not know how it would all come together but He knew. I wrote the vision down that God gave to me in 1991. Through my experiences, disappointments, pain and suffering I continued to write down everything God birthed in my spirit. Now it has finally come together.

I give due respect to ministries such as Tabernacle Missionary Baptist Church, Oak Cliff Bible Fellowship, Rising Star Missionary Baptist Church, and The Potter's House. These ministries have made an impact on my life and have aided in my growth as a Christian.

I also give the utmost respect to my grandmother Lena Taplin-Johnson who is now deceased. She taught me so much about God's word. We had countless conversations about life, about God and about family. Her background as a missionary, Sunday school teacher and seminary graduate has given me a wealth of knowledge. I am truly grateful for my paternal heritage.

I also want to thank family and friends who have shared their experiences to help strengthen me. I pray that this book will help strengthen others as I have been strengthened.

Table of Contents

Foreword

It is without hesitation that I am writing the foreword to "My Spiritual Daughter's" first book. I consider it an honor to put in writing the things that are so dear to me about Brenda.

I have watched Brenda blossom into the woman of God that she has always strive to be. Her persistence has paid off. Like the Syrophoenician woman in Mark 7:26-29, Brenda did not give up in spite of circumstances, hurts, lack, or means. Through all of this she has shown her real character. Whereas others with fewer trials than she, would have called it quits, not Brenda, she just keeps trusting God.

I believe that this book will be an inspiration to you. If you are out there struggling, falling down, messing up, and giving up, this book will help you. I believe you too with the help of the Lord and His word will get up and move forward with your life.

Finally, Brenda, you kept the course and finished writing your first book. The best is yet to come. Just remember that OUR GOD is bigger than our "messes."

Evangelist Mary Jones-Sterling

Introduction

Have you ever fell flat on your face spiritually, looked up and knew in your heart that you have disappointed God?

If we are truthful with ourselves all of us would admit that we have. For all have sinned, and come short of the glory of God. (Romans 3:23)

There will be times when you fall flat on your face during your walk with God. We often fall short because we make choices that do not line up with God's will for our lives. This is God's way of how we should do things. The Bible is His book of principles that we need to abide by to have a happy, healthy, prosperous, and fulfilling life.

Every decision that we make in life is not specifically listed in the Bible. We should still take every matter to God in prayer. Trust in the Lord with all thine heart; and lean not unto thine own understanding. In all thy ways acknowledge him, and he shall direct thy paths. (Proverbs 3:5-6)

All of us have a purpose for which God created us. Our job is to ask God what that purpose is so we can fulfill it before we leave this earth. Jeremiah is a prime example that God has a purpose for our lives. God spoke to Jeremiah saying "Before I formed thee in the belly I knew thee; and before thou cameth forth out of the womb I sanctified thee, and I ordained thee a prophet unto the nations." (Jeremiah 1:5) Jeremiah knew what his purpose in life was by talking to God. Even when we know our purpose, we still need to seek God for direction on how to fulfill it.

The only WILL that will be established and last throughout eternity is God's WILL. He will not bless, support financially, keep together or stand behind anything that is not HIS WILL for our lives. "And this is the confidence that we have in him, that, if we ask any thing according to his will, he heareth us: And if we know that he hear us, whatsoever we ask, we know that we have the petitions that we desired of him." (1 John 5:14-15)

From the cradle to the grave, life is a journey that every man has to take. It will consist of the choices we make which contribute to our life experiences, victories and defeats. The journey will also be smooth and sometimes rocky depending on our obedience and disobedience to the word of God. We have to remember that this journey is all about fulfilling the plan which God preordained for our lives.

So when we mess up and fall short of God's glory for our lives we do not have to give up and quit. There is still hope. We need to grow to the point in our lives when we sin and get off track that we confess it to God so He can help us. "If we confess our sins, he is faithful and just to forgive us our sins, and to cleanse us from all unrighteousness." (1 John 1:9)

God made provisions for our sins when He sent Jesus to die on the cross. God knew we needed a Savior that is why He sent Jesus. Even what people think are the worst of sins can be forgiven. Now there is no excuse to leave known sin un-repented. Leaving known sin un-repented leaves us open for judgment. The blood of Jesus will cover these sins. "For the wages of sin is death; but the gift of God is eternal life through Jesus Christ our Lord." (Romans 6:23)

To confess according to The Random House College Dictionary means to plead guilty. Confession to God is not reasoning and blaming your sin on someone else or convincing God that someone made you do it. Blaming others for our sins instead of dealing with ourselves really says we did not do anything wrong. This kind of confession is deception according to 1 John 1:8 "If we say that we have no sin, we deceive ourselves, and the truth is not in us." If we are serious about our walk with God, we need to get to the point when we sin that we confess to God "IT'S MY FAULT"

TAKE OWNERSHIP "IT'S MY FAULT"

Chapter I

TAKE OWNERSHIP

"IT'S MY FAULT"

When we take ownership of our sins it challenges us to evaluate our lives, our relationship with God and others. When we recognize we have sinned we need to be honest about the seriousness of our transgressions. We also need to correct the situation whenever possible. Turning away from the sins we have committed keeps us from further judgment. It also will save our very souls. Being honest about our sins and failures will help us to become more like Christ. This also helps us to work on our relationship with God.

In our relationship with God we need to make sure we are in constant fellowship with Him. We should not have any other gods before Him because He is a jealous God. (Exodus 20:3-5) We need to make sure we are studying and doing what is in His word. If we are doing anything in our personal or business lives that is wrong, we need to get it right before God has to address it.

Our relationships with others also need evaluation because God made every man in His image. God cares about the next person as much as He cares about us individually. We need to make sure that if we have sinned against someone or offended them that we get it right with them and God.

Brenda Diann Johnson

Just getting it right with God is not enough. This is evident in Matthew 5:23-24, "Therefore if thou bring thy giftto the altar, and there rememberest that thy brother hath ought against thee; Leave there thy gift before the altar, and go thy way; first be reconciled to thy brother, and then come and offer thy gift." God is not only serious about our relationship with Him but also with others. We cannot come to God with an offering unless we have made things right with our brother or sister.

Getting it right with others is important because God works through people. If you go around sinning against people and offending them knowingly, you have sinned not only against them but against God. Whether we want to admit it or not, we need people. God works through people and He uses people to bless us, give to us, care for us, love us and see about our needs.

There may be times when you have offended someone but unknowingly. In these instances, trust God to take care of them. If you become aware that you have offended someone go and make things right. Sometimes an apology will suffice. In other instances you may need to pray and ask God how to make things right with someone you have offended or sinned against. It is important to always wait for God's direction because you do not want to be misunderstood or give place to the devil.

It is important that we keep our relationships right with others. Keeping in mind that no one is perfect. People sin against us and we sin against people. Our forgiveness from God depends on our forgiveness of others. According to verse 12 in Matthew 6, "And forgive us our debts, as we forgive our debtors," shows that Jesus model prayer is how we should approach God even when we pray. It also shows that when we come to God and ask for forgiveness of our sins, we also have to make sure we have forgiven others of their sins against us.

Even though we have failed in some areas of our lives God will still cause all things to work together according to Romans 8:28. Therefore whatever mistakes you have made, there is FORGIVENESS AND JUSTICE.

Brenda Diann Johnson

Personal Testimony...................

When I was a student in college I made a failing grade on a test. I did not study enough to know the material. I could not blame anyone but myself. I had to admit that it was my fault.

Prayer..........

Dear Father thank you for allowing me the privilege to come into your presence again. Father I repent of my sins. Those that I know about and those I may have forgotten. Father help me be more like you and ultimately conformed to the image of your son.

Help me Lord to be more transparent with you and others in admitting my sins. Help me not to hide from you and to boldly confess where I have went wrong. Help me to hide your word in my heart so I will not sin against you. Lord I love you and I want to be right in your sight.

Help me to take ownership for the things that I do. Please bring godly people in my life to hold me accountable so that I may grow to spiritual maturity. In Jesus Name, Amen

Further Study..........

If we confess our sins, he is faithful and just to forgive us our sins, and to cleanse us from all unrighteousness. (1 John 1:9)

Search me, O God, and know my heart: try me, and know my thoughts: And see if there be any wicked way in me, and lead me in the way everlasting. (Psalms 139:23-24)

Thy word have I hid in mine heart, that I might not sin against thee. (Psalms 119:11)

For godly sorrow worketh repentance to salvation not to be repented of: but the sorrow of the world worketh death. (2 Corinthians 7:10)

Blessed are the pure in heart: for they shall see God. (Matthew 5:8)

For I acknowledge my transgressions: and my sin is ever before me. Against thee, thee only, have I sinned, and done this evil in thy sight: that thou mightest be justified when thou speakest, and be clear when thou judgest. (Psalms 51:3-4)

Now therefore thus saith the Lord of hosts; Consider your ways. Ye have sown much, and bring in little; ye eat, but ye have not enough; ye drink, but ye are not filled with drink; ye clothe you, but there is none warm; and he that earneth wages earneth wages to put it into a bag with holes. Thus saith the Lord of hosts; Consider your ways. (Haggai 1:5-7)

Brenda Diann Johnson

It is good for me that I have been afflicted; that I might learn thy statutes. (Psalms 119:71)

For if we would judge ourselves, we should not be judged. But when we are judged, we are chastened of the Lord, that we should not be condemned with the world. (1 Corinthians 11:31-32)

He that covereth his sins shall not prosper: but whoso confesseth and forsaketh them shall have mercy. (Proverbs 28:13)

FORGIVENESS AND JUSTICE

Chapter II

FORGIVENESS AND JUSTICE

God has promised us forgiveness if we confess our sins to Him according to 1 John 1:9. He loves us unconditionally and wants the best for us. He showed this AGAPE love when He sent His son Jesus Christ to die for our sins. God wanted a sacrifice that would justify the penalty for sin. "For the wages of sin is death; but the gift of God is eternal life through Jesus Christ our Lord." (Romans 6:23)

Even though God forgives us, we must recognize that He is also a God of justice. Justice according to the Random House College Dictionary is the administering of deserved punishment or reward. Because God is just He will administer punishment or reward to anyone when necessary. He also has the absolute authority to administer this justice how He deems necessary. God knows what degree of punishment and reward each of us need. We can count on God to punish us when we sin and go astray. He will also reward or recompense us when we suffer a wrong done to us. Therefore forgiveness and justice go hand and hand.

God wants everything done decent and in order. (1 Corinthians 14:40) He is the creator of everything that exists. He ordained and created government according to Romans 13:1. For every law there is a consequence for breaking it. This is true in any legal form of government. There has to be order when dealing with the rule of people.

Brenda Diann Johnson

The pros and cons of any set of laws should guarantee
fairness to everyone. This is also true when it comes to the
laws or principles God had established in the beginning. In
Deuteronomy chapter 28 God outlines the blessings and
curses for obeying and disobeying His commands. God told
the Israelites if they obeyed He would bless them in the city
and bless them in the field.

God is concerned about us. He does not want us
separated from Him because of sin. He was very specific in
the beginning when He created Adam and Eve. He gave
specific instructions of what to do and not to do. He also
made provisions for Adam and Eve so they could be happy.
It was disobedience to what God said that later got them
evicted from the garden of Eden. (Genesis 3:23-24) Even
though God loved Adam and Eve He still had to administer
justice because of their disobedience. God cursed the ground
and said Adam would work it in toil and eat of it all the days
of his life. (Genesis 3:17) For Eve, God said He would
multiply her child bearing pains and that her desire will be
for her husband and her husband will rule over her. (Genesis
3:16)

Many times we talk about receiving forgiveness of our
sins but we do not want to talk about the consequences of sin.
Consequences must come as a result of disobedience and sin.
God has set a standard by which we must live our lives. He
is serious about the effects of sin. He is not playing. He
even warns us in Galatians 6:7 "Be not deceived; God is not

mocked: for whatsoever a man soweth, that shall he also reap." This is the very reason why we need to be careful of what we say and do. If we do not want to reap a harvest of injustice then we should not sow injustice toward anyone. God also warns "For he that soweth to his flesh shall of the flesh reap corruption; but he that soweth to the spirit shall of the spirit reap life everlasting." (Galatians 6:8)

Even though God has provided the blood of His son to cover sin, we need to be careful of abusing the use of it. God makes this very clear in Hebrews 10:26-27. "For if we sin wilfully after that we have received the knowledge of the truth, there remaineth no more sacrifice for sins, but a certain fearful looking for of judgment and fiery indignation, which shall devour the adversaries." We need to make sure when we repent and ask for forgiveness we mean it. It should not be lip service but it should be heart service. We should have godly sorrow for our sins. This kind of godly sorrow brings true repentance. (2 Corinthians 7:10)

Sometimes we do not realize we are playing Russian roulette when we repent, ask for forgiveness and plead the blood over our sins, knowing we do not mean it. We want forgiveness, protection under the blood of Jesus and still practice our sin. In short, we want to have our cake and eat it too.

God is omniscient and He is able to discern what is really going on with us. He will expose us. God knows when we are trying to play games with Him and His Son. He knows when we are using and abusing the blood of the lamb. If we are guilty of this, punishment will be worse for us because we have trodden under foot the son of God and hath counted the blood of the covenant that sanctified us as an unholy thing. This is insulting the spirit of grace. (Hebrews 10:29) We must reverence God and take His laws seriously. "It is a fearful thing to fall into the hands of the living God." (Hebrews 10:31) God will judge sin no matter where it is and no matter who is at fault. When God arises His enemies will have to scatter. (Psalms 68:1)

God knows that we will miss the mark from time to time. When we are trying our best to please Him we may miss the mark. According to Isaiah 64:6 even our righteousness is as filthy rags before Him. This is all the more reason to obey God and choose His way of doing things. We can not be right within ourselves. Just like David, we can confess that we were brought forth in iniquity, and in sin we were conceived. (Psalms 51:5) Since we know that we are as sheep and need a shepherd it is better for us to obey. "To do justice and judgment is more acceptable to the Lord than sacrifice." (Proverbs 21:3)

God wants us to be victorious. He wants us to have a full and abundant life. This is why He warns us ahead of time about what sin will do and how it will affect us long and short term. God warned the Israelites not to repeat the sins of their fathers. (Ezekiel 20:18) He also warned them of not serving idols. He said He would visit the iniquity of the fathers upon the children, unto the third and fourth generations. (Exodus 20:5) This would be a long term effect of sin. Some know these sins as generational curses. Sins that continue generation after generation. Whatever the generational curses are we should desire to do better than our parents, grandparents, or great-grandparents did. Each generation should get wiser and have more knowledge than the previous generation.

Short term results of sin are immediate. Sometimes the consequences come right away shortly after the sin committed. We are in control of our actions when we decide to disobey. Unfortunately we are not in control of the consequences that come as a result of sin. We are prey to the bad things that will happen to us. God will always show how serious He is about sin. An example of a short term result of sin would be the story of Ananias and Sapphira. This husband and wife team immediately fell dead because they lied about some property they sold. (Acts 5:1-11)

Another short and long term result of sin would include the story of David and Bathsheba. As a result of their adulterous relationship and the murder of Uriah, God issued a short term and long term punishment. The child conceived in the adulterous relationship was born sick and shortly died. God also promised the sword would never depart from David's house because of his evil deed. (2 Samuel 12:10-18) The long term punishment for the Israelites kept them from seeing the promised land. They were in the wilderness for 40 years. Because of their continuous sins God only allowed their children to see the promised land. (Joshua 5:6-9) There are many things that could happen as a result of sin if we do not correct our behavior and lifestyle.

Consequences serve as a reminder of what we did wrong. They remind us not to be disobedient to God's word. We become mindful that we could inevitably get a result we do not like. A result that will hurt us emotionally, spiritually, or physically. Consequences are necessary to keep us from going astray or going down the wrong road again.

Even though God has to punish where He finds sins, He also recompenses for wrongs we have suffered. We are all responsible for our actions and the deeds that we do. We are accountable for what we do to others. No one likes it when they suffer a wrong at the hand of another. We want respect, care, and love. Unfortunately sin overtakes us from time to time and we hurt others with our actions. It is good to know that God loves justice. He will punish our enemies for the wrong they have perpetrated on us.

God will not let us be put to shame. Jeremiah was confident that God would handle his enemies when he said "O Lord, thou knowest: remember me, and visit me, and revenge me of my persecutors; take me not away in thy longsuffering: know that for thy sake I have suffered rebuke." (Jeremiah 15:15)

God will also give us back what the enemy stole from us with interest. This is demonstrated in the book of Job. Job was tried by the enemy and went through a test that God allowed. The enemy attacked Job's health, finances and family. At the end of the test God gave Job more than he had before. (Job 42:10-17) Whatever wrong you may have suffered God will make sure you receive justice. According to Proverbs 11:1, "A false balance is an abomination to the Lord: but a just weight is His delight." God will balance the scales. He is just and will pay back trouble to those who trouble you. He will give relief to those who are troubled. (2 Thessalonians 1:6-7)

So whatever our enemies may do to us we can rest in knowing vengeance belong to God. He will repay according to Romans 12:19. Instead of retaliating we should obey God and love our enemies, do good to them which hate us, bless them that curse us, and pray for them which despitefully use us. (Luke 6:27-28) When we choose to do the latter instead of retaliating it will keep us from falling under judgment.

Now that we have forgiveness and have a clear understanding of justice we can move forward into our destiny. The very sin that we have been delivered from WATCH GOD USE IT!

Brenda Diann Johnson

Personal Testimony...................

    I had to ask God for forgiveness after I went through a terrible divorce. God reminded me that I must live by His standard. I did not wait for God to choose my spouse. The relationship ended in divorce. God warns us not to be unequally yoked together with unbelievers. Righteousness does not have fellowship with unrighteousness. Light does not commune with darkness. Christ and Belial will not be in agreement nor a believer with an infidel. (2 Corinthians 6:14-15) God did not leave me in my condition. He had a different destiny for me.

Prayer............

    Heavenly Father thank you for loving me enough to send Jesus, your son, to die for my sins. Thank you for providing forgiveness even though I am not worthy. I recognize that it is you that make me worthy.

    Cover me Lord with the blood of Jesus to wash away my sins. Help me Lord to immediately repent before you when I am aware that I have sinned. I need your forgiveness every day. Help me Lord to forgive others when they have sinned against me. Help me not to hold any grudges and to freely release others that have wronged me. I know in forgiving others you in turn will freely forgive me for my wrong doings. Help me choose to love instead of hate. Help me to accept your righteous judgment when I am punished. I know that your judgment is right and justice must take place when I sin against you or my neighbor. Remind me Lord to pray for my enemies when they are doing wicked things to me. Help me to hold my hand back from vengeance and remember that vengeance belongs to you.

Lord help me to be humble when judgment is taking place against my enemies. Keep my heart soft so that it will be full of love and forgiveness. Help me not to become bitter and to keep the door open for those who want to come back to make things right with me. In Jesus Name, Amen.

Brenda Diann Johnson

Further Study

Forgiveness.........

But I say unto you, Love your enemies, bless them that curse you, do good to them that hate you, and pray for them which despitefully use you, and persecute you; That ye may be the children of your Father which is in heaven: for he maketh his sun to rise on the evil and on the good, and sendeth rain on the just and on the unjust. (Matthew 5:44-45)

And when ye stand praying, forgive, if ye have ought against any: that your Father also which is in heaven may forgive you your trespasses. But if ye do not forgive, neither will your Father which is in heaven forgive your trespasses. (Mark 11:25-26)

Therefore if thine enemy hunger, feed him; if he thirst, give him drink: for in so doing thou shalt heap coals of fire on his head. (Romans 12:20)

Say not thou, I will recompense evil; but wait on the Lord, and he shall save thee. (Proverbs 20:22)

If we confess our sins, he is faithful and just to forgive us our sins, and to cleanse us from all unrighteousness. (1 John 1:9)

Bless the Lord, O my soul, and forget not all his benefits: Who forgiveth all thine iniquities; who healeth all thy diseases; Who redeemeth thy life from destruction; who crowneth thee with lovingkindness and tender mercies. (Psalms 103:2-4)

Christ hath redeemed us from the curse of the law, being made a curse for us: for it is written, Cursed is every one that hangeth on a tree. (Galatians 3:13)

Justice........

For whom the Lord loveth he correcteth; even as a father the son in whom he delighteth. (Proverbs 3:12)

Behold, happy is the man whom God correcteth: therefore despise not thou the chastening of the Almighty: For he maketh sore, and bindeth up: he woundeth, and his hands make whole. (Job 5:17-18)

Blessed is the man whom thou chastenest, O Lord, and teachest him out of thy law; that thou mayest give him rest from the days of adversity, until the pit be digged for the wicked. (Psalms 94:12-13)

But when we are judged, we are chastened of the Lord, that we should not be condemned with the world. (1 Corinthians 11:32)

For whom the Lord loveth he chasteneth, and scourgeth every son whom he receiveth. If ye endure chastening, God dealeth with you as with sons; for what son is he whom the father chasteneth not? (Hebrews 12:6-7)

For they verily for a few days chastened us after their own pleasure; but he for our profit, that we might be partakers of his holiness. Now no chastening for the present seemeth to be joyous, but grievous: nevertheless afterward it yieldeth the peaceable fruit of righteousness unto them which are exercised thereby. (Hebrews 12:10-11)

For the wages of sin is death; but the gift of God is eternal life through Jesus Christ our Lord. (Romans 6:23)

Who gave himself for our sins, that he might deliver us from this present evil world, according to the will of God and our Father. (Galatians 1:4)

For the Lord God is a sun and shield: the Lord will give grace and glory: no good thing will he withhold from them that walk uprightly. (Psalms 84:11)

For he that eateth and drinketh unworthily, eateth and drinketh damnation to himself, not discerning the Lord's body. For this cause many are weak and sickly among you, and many sleep. For if we would judge ourselves, we should not be judged. But when we are judged, we are chastened of the Lord, that we should not be condemned with the world. (1 Corinthians 11:29-32)

But God is the judge: he putteth down one, and setteth up another. (Psalms 75:7)

For if we sin wilfully after that we have received the knowledge of the truth, there remaineth no more sacrifice for sins, But a certain fearful looking for of judgment and fiery indignation, which shall devour the adversaries. (Hebrews 10:26-27)

And even as they did not like to retain God in their knowledge, God gave them over to a reprobate mind, to do those things which are not convenient. (Romans 1:28)

The Lord shall send upon thee cursing, vexation, and rebuke, in all that thou settest thine hand unto for to do, until thou be destroyed, and until thou perish quickly; because of the wickedness of thy doings, whereby thou hast forsaken me. (Deuteronomy 28:20)

Be not deceived; God is not mocked: for whatsoever a man soweth, that shall he also reap. (Galatians 6:7)

He that hath a froward heart findeth no good: and he that hath a perverse tongue falleth into mischief. (Proverbs 17:20)

Good understanding giveth favour: but the way of transgressors is hard. (Proverbs 13:15)

But the wicked are like the troubled sea, when it cannot rest, whose waters cast up mire and dirt. There is no peace, saith my God, to the wicked. (Isaiah 57:20-21)

For the eyes of the Lord are over the righteous, and his ears are open unto their prayers: but the face of the Lord is against them that do evil. (1 Peter 3:12)

The Lord shall cause thine enemies that rise up against thee to be smitten before thy face: they shall come out against thee one way, and flee before thee seven ways. (Deuteronomy 28:7)

Brenda Diann Johnson

When a man's ways please the Lord, he maketh even his enemies to be at peace with him. (Proverbs 16:7)

WATCH GOD USE IT

Chapter III

WATCH GOD USE IT

Fiery trials will come in your life whether you are a believer or non believer. It does not matter if you are spiritually mature or if you had many victories in the past. You will have trials and more trials so get ready. According to Psalm 34:19, "Many are the afflictions of the righteous: but the Lord delivereth him out of them all." This is a comfort to the believer because life is many times unpredictable. No matter what trouble believers have God is still with them. "When thou passest through the waters, I will be with thee; and through the rivers, they shall not overflow thee: when thou walkest through the fire, thou shalt not be burned; neither shall the flame kindle upon thee, for I am the Lord thy God..." (Isaiah 43:2-3)

God will deliver you in every trial and tribulation. He will also deliver others while you go through your tests. God wants to make Himself known to you so you will trust Him. He also makes Himself known to others who watch you go through your trial. Others can see in whom you trust when they witness how you handle your trial. Your walk and your talk exhibit how you handle your trial. Both must line up with the word of God. We are not perfect and sometimes we become discouraged. Our discouragement may show in our walk and talk. This is ok, as long as we stay on track with God. People can see if the majority of our walk and talk lines up with God's word. He wants us to be a witness for

Brenda Diann Johnson

Him and He wants to show His power through us. Greater is He who is in you than he who is in the world. (1 John 4:4)

God also wants us to minister to others when we have overcome our painful trials. He will send others your way to get what they need and receive encouragement. We should comfort others with the same comfort that God once comforted us with. (2 Corinthians 1:4)

There are times when God wants us to minister to others while we are going through our painful trials. He wants others to see that even though we are believers we have struggles too. We feel pain from the wounds we experience in life. He also wants others to see that we become discouraged, fail and sometimes miss the mark too. Even when we fail we still overcome our trials and get the victory. We can do all things through Christ who strengthens us. (Philippians 4:13)

Some trials we encounter will not be for others to see. Some are private between the believer and God. When God chooses to display us on trial, He has a purpose for it. God wants to develop our faith as well as others. Others can also see the practical things that believers do to walk through a trial while keeping faith in God. We should also obey God's direction in every step that we take. This is important because Christianity is not magic. It is a lifestyle the believer lives by faith and obedience to the word of God. "But without faith it is impossible to please him: for he that cometh to God must believe that he is, and that he is a rewarder of them that diligently seek him." (Hebrews 11:6)

Now we know that we must live by faith to please God. How do we know if we are walking in the right direction? We must ASK GOD FOR DIRECTION.

Brenda Diann Johnson

Personal Testimony.....................

Being the first to get a college degree in my family helped to inspire other family members to go back to college. It also inspired those younger than me to go to college. I endured college through the death of family members, disappointments, and hard times.

Prayer.....................

Dear Father thank you for comforting me during my trials and tribulations. Thank you for trusting me to endure the trials that have been assigned to me. Thank you for teaching me and building my character during the time of trouble.

I want you to mold me into what you ordained me to be from the beginning of time. Whatever it takes to bring out your glory in me I submit to you wholeheartedly.

Thank you for using me as an example to others when I go through appointed tests. When others are watching help me to have a good attitude while you are working on me. Let my witness be powerful so others may learn to trust you. Help me to witness and use my testimony to tell others about you. Let me be faithful in telling others how you will deliver out of trouble.

Give me wisdom of when to share and not to share during the times you are changing me. Thank you for helping me to be an over comer by the blood of the lamb and by the word of my testimony. (Revelation 12:11) In Jesus Name, Amen.

Further Study...........

For I know the thoughts that I think toward you, saith the Lord, thoughts of peace, and not of evil, to give you an expected end. (Jeremiah 29:11)

Ye are of God, little children, and have overcome them: because greater is he that is in you, than he that is in the world. (1 John 4:4)

How should one chase a thousand, and two put ten thousand to flight, except their rock had sold them, and the Lord had shut them up? (Deuteronomy 32:30)

Then he answered and spake unto me, saying, This is the word of the Lord unto Zerubbabel, saying, Not by might, nor by power, but by my spirit, saith the Lord of hosts. (Zechariah 4:6)

And he said, Hearken ye, all Judah, and ye inhabitants of Jerusalem, and thou king Jehoshaphat, Thus saith the Lord unto you, Be not afraid nor dismayed by reason of this great multitude; for the battle is not yours, but God's. (2 Chronicles 20:15)

For the eyes of the Lord run to and fro throughout the whole earth, to shew himself strong in the behalf of them whose heart is perfect toward him. (2 Chronicles 16:9)

So shall my word be that goeth forth out of my mouth: it shall not return unto me void, but it shall accomplish that which I please, and it shall prosper in the thing whereto I sent it. (Isaiah 55:11)

Then said the Lord unto me, Thou hast well seen: for I will hasten my word to perform it. (Jeremiah 1:12)

Fear not, little flock; for it is your Father's good pleasure to give you the kingdom. (Luke 12:32)

Let them shout for joy, and be glad, that favour my righteous cause: yea, let them say continually, Let the Lord be magnified, which hath pleasure in the prosperity of his servant. (Psalm 35:27)

And Joseph said unto them, Fear not: for am I in the place of God? But as for you, ye thought evil against me; but God meant it unto good, to bring to pass, as it is this day, to save much people alive. (Genesis 50:19-20)

And we know that all things work together for good to them that love God, to them who are the called according to his purpose. (Romans 8:28)

It is he that sitteth upon the circle of the earth, and the inhabitants thereof are as grasshoppers; that stretcheth out the heavens as a curtain, and spreadeth them out as a tent to dwell in: That bringeth the princes to nothing; he maketh the judges of the earth as vanity. (Isaiah 40:22-23)

I waited patiently for the Lord; and he inclined unto me, and heard my cry. He brought me up also out of an horrible pit, out of the miry clay, and set my feet upon a rock, and established my goings. And he hath put a new song in my mouth, even praise unto our God: many shall see it, and fear, and shall trust in the Lord. (Psalm 40:1-3)

And they overcame him by the blood of the Lamb, and by the word of their testimony; and they loved not their lives unto the death. (Revelation 12:11)

No weapon that is formed against thee shall prosper; and every tongue that shall rise against thee in judgment thou shalt condemn. This is the heritage of the servants of the Lord, and their righteousness is of me, saith the Lord. (Isaiah 54:17)

ASK FOR DIRECTION

Chapter IV

ASK FOR DIRECTION

God gives us direction when we pray. The Holy Spirit guides and leads us if we are walking after the spirit and not the flesh. God's direction is in the Holy Bible. He gives direction to us through other people and through circumstances whether good or bad.

It is important to pray without ceasing. (1 Thessalonians 5:17) We should pray to God when we are unsure about which direction to go or what step to take. We should also pray according to His word and expect an answer. We have this promise according to 1 John 5:14-16, "And this is the confidence that we have in him, that, if we ASK ANYTHING ACCORDING TO HIS WILL, He heareth us: And if we know that He hear us, whatsoever we ask, we know that we have the petitions that we desired of him."

Therefore we must question ourselves whether we really want God's will manifested in our lives. We cannot pray for anything that we know is contrary to HIS WILL because He will have a deaf ear to it. There are times when we may not know if we are praying contrary to the will of God for our lives. God has also made a provision for us even in our ignorance. According to Romans 8:26-27, "Likewise the Spirit also helpeth our infirmities: for we know not what we should pray for as we ought: but the Spirit itself maketh intercession for us with groanings which cannot be uttered.

Brenda Diann Johnson

And he that searcheth the hearts knoweth what is the mind of the Spirit, because he maketh intercession for the saints ACCORDING TO THE WILL OF GOD."

When we pray the Holy Spirit understands what we mean when our thoughts and words do not come out right. The Holy Spirit will intercede for us in our prayers only according to the will of God and not according to our will. The Holy Spirit also leads us in our daily lives. The Spirit helps us to make the right decisions by bringing God's word to our remembrance. The Spirit also gives us discernment when making decisions or how to handle a situation.

The Holy Spirit protects us and warns us of danger. God quickens our spirit so He can speak directly to us. God also use people to warn us and to confirm what He said when He quickened our spirit. The Holy Spirit grieves when we do things that are not in line with God's will. Our conscience will let us know that something is wrong with us, the choice that we have made, or about a situation in our lives.

God leads us through people to let us know if we are walking in the right direction. The people God use will give us the answers we asked for in our prayers. It is so important to seek worthy and godly counsel. "Where no counsel is, the people fall: but in the multitude of counsellors there is safety." (Proverbs 11:14) We should seek counsel from people who will tell us what is right. This will help us make a final decision that is right and pleasing to God.

God also leads through His word. No matter what problems we have, God's word will have the answer to our situation. We should obey His principles. If we obey and apply His principles we will get the promised results in His word. If we do not obey His word we will also suffer judgment. So therefore, to obey is better than sacrifice. (1Samuel 15:22)

Circumstances also have a way of leading us the right or wrong way. Some call it trial and error. Our circumstances whether good or bad are indicators of the decisions we made. If we end up in good circumstances we made a good decision and if we end up with bad circumstances then we made a bad decision. This is generally how the rule goes and sometimes there may be a few exceptions to the rule. In either case circumstances will help us go the right way, especially if we want God's best. You cannot enjoy God's best for your life if you are always stumbling into bad circumstances.

When we study God's Word, walk in the Spirit, and listen to godly counsel we will not keep stumbling in life. We begin to have wisdom. Wisdom according to The Random House College Dictionary means knowledge of what is true or right coupled with good judgment. God's word gives us wisdom and is the road map to a successful Christian life. When we obtain wisdom and discretion, God's word says "then shalt thou walk in thy way safely, and thy foot shall not stumble." (Proverbs 3:23)

Brenda Diann Johnson

Once you have asked God for direction in your life and He gives it to you, DON'T KEEP WALKING IN THE WRONG DIRECTION! Turn around and get back on track. When God has shown you an area of compromise in your life, don't keep compromising in that area. When you have compromised God's word and made a mess of everything, now it is TIME TO MAKE BETTER CHOICES.

Personal Testimony....................

When I was a senior in high school I had to decide which college I would attend. I also had to decide which direction or career path I would take. When I prayed about it, God helped me decide on a communications major.

Prayer....................

Heavenly Father I come before you recognizing that you are Omnipresent. You are able to be everywhere at the same time. I reverence you and trust your advice on which direction I need to go in life.

I cannot see what is ahead of me and I need you to be my eyes. You are able to see further than me and can direct me on which way to go. Help me to acknowledge you in all my ways and you shall direct my paths. (Proverbs 3:6)

When I get off course with the destiny you have ordained for me please help me to get back on track. Help me to stay on track by avoiding pitfalls the enemy has for me.

Help me to stay focused on the things that are important to my destiny. Keep me from distractions that will cause me to wander off your path for my life. Help me to walk by faith while trusting you to direct me. In Jesus Name, Amen.

Brenda Diann Johnson

Further Study......

If any of you lack wisdom, let him ask of God, that giveth to all men liberally, and upbraideth not; and it shall be given him. (James 1:5)

Trust in the Lord with all thine heart; and lean not unto thine own understanding. In all thy ways acknowledge him, and he shall direct thy paths. (Proverbs 3:5-6)

Be careful for nothing; but in everything by prayer and supplication with thanksgiving let your requests be made known unto God. And the peace of God, which passeth all understanding, shall keep your hearts and minds through Christ Jesus. (Philippians 4:6-7)

The steps of a good man are ordered by the Lord: and he delighteth in his way. (Psalms 37:23)

Seek ye the Lord while he may be found, call ye upon him while he is near: (Isaiah 55:6)

There is a way that seemeth right unto a man, but the end thereof are the ways of death. (Proverbs 16:25)

Be still, and know that I am God: I will be exalted among the heathen, I will be exalted in the earth. (Psalms 46:10)

Thy word is a lamp unto my feet, and a light unto my path. (Psalms 119:105)

And thine ears shall hear a word behind thee, saying, This is the way, walk ye in it, when ye turn to the right hand, and when ye turn to the left. (Isaiah 30:21)

I will instruct thee and teach thee in the way which thou shalt go: I will guide thee with mine eye. (Psalm 32:8)

The righteousness of the perfect shall direct his way: but the wicked shall fall by his own wickedness. (Proverbs 11:5)

For his God doth instruct him to discretion, and doth teach him. (Isaiah 28:26)

A man's heart deviseth his way: but the Lord directeth his steps. (Proverbs 16:9)

For this God is our God forever and ever: he will be our guide even unto death. (Psalms 48:14)

I must work the works of him that sent me, while it is day: the night cometh, when no man can work. (John 9:4)

MAKE BETTER CHOICES

Chapter V

MAKE BETTER CHOICES

Making better choices in our lives is a process that all Christians learn to do. Many times the choices that we make stem from a variety of things that influence us. These choices sometimes stem from our background, parental guidance, our family beliefs, traditions, attitudes and culture. The way we did things in our families before we were saved was ok because it worked for our family. It was the way we functioned.

Before you were born into this world God chose you. (Ephesians 1:3-5) God chose your family, your parents, your background, your economic status, your personality, your talents, your traits, your past, present, and your future. God knew which direction you would take and your choices. He even knew the reasoning behind your decisions. He also knew the very thing that would bring you to Christ. He knew who would choose Him and who would not. Even though God knew all of this before the foundation of the world, He still made provisions for all to come unto Him. The choice is yours.

According to Deuteronomy 30:19 God says "I call heaven and earth to record this day against you, that I have set before you life and death, blessing and cursing: therefore choose life, that both thou and thy seed may live." God made provisions for us TO KNOW HIM through creation, His law, and His prophets. God showed us AGAPE LOVE when He sent Jesus to die on a cross for the sins of the world. God wanted to make sure that all ground was covered so we would be without excuse when it came to knowing Him. (Romans 1:20-21)

God knew well in advance that everyone would have issues based on their past, background, experiences, upbringing, etc. He tells us in Philippians 2:12 to work out our own salvation with fear and trembling. You and God are the only two that really know what issues you must work through to become conformed to Christ's image. God already knew that we needed a savior because there is a lot wrong with each and every one of us. God sent His only begotten son to die for our sins while we were yet sinners. (Romans 5:8)

Once you accept Christ as your savior, it is up to you to make changes in your life to line up with God's word. According to Romans 12:2, we are no longer to be conformed to this world but to be transformed by the renewing of our minds.

We must also work out our own salvation everyday with fear and trembling. I believe we need to do this with fear and trembling because we have developed habits over the years that will be difficult to break. We may have done them out of ignorance and not knowing those habits are against the word of God. Little by little God shows us what is wrong with us. He exposes things that we need to change in our lives. We need to fear God enough that when He shows us where to change we do it. We also do it because it disappoints Him. God is so merciful to us and He is patient with us. I believe if He showed us everything that was wrong with us at one time, we would have a heart attack. We could not handle it. God is patient with us. He shows us what we need to change in our lives when he feels we can handle it. God is also a just God as well. He will chastise us when we refuse to change those things He has continually spoken to us about.

God knows our hearts and He is also very aware of the schemes of the devil. His mission is to kill, steal and destroy. Many times we want to make better choices. We want to live the way God wants us to live, but we get tricked time and time again by our adversary the devil. Satan does not come to us when we are strong, he comes to us when we are weak. Satan continues to sneak in on every believer at one time or another. Satan comes when we are weak and vulnerable; inexperienced, naive, and young; in need, and when we have to make major decisions that can either make or break us.

Believers at one time or another have been weak and vulnerable because of an incident that has taken place in their lives. The incident may have been the loss of a loved one, divorce, an accident, or illness. These things can leave us prey to Satan. Our adversary, the devil, walks around as a roaring lion seeking whom he may devour. (1 Peter 5:8)

Brenda Diann Johnson

When we are weak we can't make the right decisions and we can easily be manipulated. When we are vulnerable to the enemy we need to stay in constant prayer and ask God to hide us and keep us safe from the enemy. (Psalms 61:1-4) We should also ask other prayer warriors to pray for us. This is important because sometimes we are too weak to pray for ourselves.

Satan is also able to trick us when we are inexperienced in some areas of life. He also comes when we are young and naive. Satan knows what we do not have knowledge of and will entice us in areas where we are ignorant. Satan has been around longer than we have and knows every way to trick man. When we are young, naive and inexperienced it is easy for Satan to trick us. We have not lived long enough to know Satan's devices. It is good news to know that God has been around even longer than Satan. God knows Satan's schemes, tricks and devices. Therefore a young person who lacks wisdom should ask God who gives to all men liberally, and upbraideth not; and it shall be given him. (James 1:5) God has control over everything that concerns heaven and earth. His son Jesus is the author and finisher of our faith and Satan's fate. (Hebrews 12:2; Revelation 20:10)

Satan also comes to trick us when we are in need, lack, or when we want something. Satan loves to find someone in desperate need who will do anything to get their needs met illegally, immorally, and ungodly. Esau was a good example of someone being in desperate need and fulfilling his need illegally. He was also tricked by his brother Jacob to give up his birthright according to Genesis 25:29-34. Satan does not want us to wait on God to supply all our needs according to his riches in glory by Christ Jesus. (Philippians 4:19) The devil wants us to rush and make a quick decision to meet our own needs. When we do not wait to see how God would have worked it out for us we miss out on His very best. When we need something we should pray and ask God for his provisions. We need to be patient and be still. According to Psalm 46:10 God says "Be still, and know that I am God" He wants us to trust Him.

Our need could be money, food, shelter, clothing, employment, or a need to be loved. God will meet all of these needs in the appropriate time He has allotted for them to be met. He is working out things behind the scenes. He is gathering the right resources, lining up the right people, changing hearts, getting ready to increase your finances and making all grace abound unto you. This is why we must have faith and not waver in times of need, lack, and want. He is working all things together for good to them that love Him. If you love Him you don't have to worry. The question you need to ask yourself is, Do you love Him? Do you belong to Him? For the righteous have never been forsaken nor his seed begging bread. (Psalms 37:25)

Satan also comes to deceive us when we have to make major decisions in our lives. Major decisions could include

Brenda Diann Johnson

marriage, where you will live, where you will worship, job choices, business decisions, or decisions for your children. Satan comes to trick us in this area because he knows a wrong decision can have a long term affect on us and those involved. When making major decisions we need to first pray about them and ask God for directions. We need to do our necessary research and seek worthy counsel before making our final decision. If we do this, we are moving toward making better decisions in our lives. We need to be careful in making hasty decisions because we have to deal with the end results. Some wrong decisions can easily be fixed, some can be fixed over time, and some can never be fixed. We need to calculate the cost before putting our final stamp of approval on it. God wants us to walk in victory and He wants us to succeed in doing His will.

Now that you are aware of Satan's schemes and have learned how to make better choices, it is time to WALK IN TRUTH.

Personal Testimony............

Once I made a bad choice buying a car. I allowed a car dealer to talk me into getting a car with unknown problems. I did not pray about it and suffered for the choice I made. I had car problems shortly after I signed the contract. Now I do my research when it comes to making major purchases and I seek God first in major decisions.

Prayer................

Dear Father thank you for being Omniscient. You know everything and your knowledge is great. I need you to help me make better decisions in my life. I recognize that my knowledge is limited to what is on earth but you are able to give me wisdom.

Your wisdom is not like man's. Your ways are not my ways and your thoughts are not my thoughts. You said in James 1:5 "If any of you lack wisdom, let him ask of God that giveth to all men liberally, and upbraideth not; and it shall be given him."

Right now I am asking you for wisdom on how to handle my day to day situations and problems. Help me to seek you first when I have a problem whether big or small. Help me to remember if I come to you first and obtain your wisdom I will get the victory every time. In Jesus Name, Amen.

Brenda Diann Johnson

Further Study.......

Therefore to him that knoweth to do good, and doeth it not, to him it is sin. (James 4:17)

I call heaven and earth to record this day against you, that I have set before you life and death, blessing and cursing: therefore choose life, that both thou and thy seed may live. (Deuteronomy 30:19)

If ye be willing and obedient, ye shall eat the good of the land: But if ye refuse and rebel, ye shall be devoured with the sword: for the mouth of the Lord hath spoken it. (Isaiah 1:19-20)

And all these blessings shall come on thee, and overtake thee, if thou shalt hearken unto the voice of the Lord thy God. Blessed shalt thou be in the city, and blessed shalt thou be in the field. (Deuteronomy 28:2-3)

Blessed is the man that walketh not in the counsel of the ungodly, nor standeth in the way of sinners, nor sitteth in the seat of the scornful. But his delight is in the law of the Lord; and in his law doth he meditate day and night. (Psalms 1:1-2)

But seek ye first the kingdom of God, and his righteousness, and all these things shall be added unto you. (Matthew 6:33)

Honour thy father and thy mother: and, Thou shalt love thy neighbour as thyself. (Matthew 19:19)

But I say unto you, Love your enemies, bless them that curse you, do good to them that hate you, and pray for them which despitefully use you, and persecute you; That ye may be the children of your Father which is in heaven: for he maketh his sun to rise on the evil and on the good, and sendeth rain on the just and on the unjust. (Matthew 5:44-45)

Bless them which persecute you: bless, and curse not. (Romans 12:14)

If it be possible, as much as lieth in you, live peaceably with all men. (Romans 12:18)

Let your conversation be without covetousness; and be content with such things as ye have: for he hath said, I will never leave thee, nor forsake thee. (Hebrews 13:5)

Give not that which is holy unto the dogs, neither cast ye your pearls before swine, lest they trample them under their feet, and turn again and rend you. (Matthew 7:6)

Be not deceived: evil communications corrupt good manners. (1 Corinthians 15:33)

Study to shew thyself approved unto God, a workman that needeth not to be ashamed, rightly dividing the word of truth. (2 Timothy 2:15)

Not rendering evil for evil, or railing for railing: but contrariwise blessing; knowing that ye are thereunto called, that ye should inherit a blessing. (1 Peter 3:9)

Brenda Diann Johnson

For he that will love life, and see good days, let him refrain his tongue from evil, and his lips that they speak no guile:Let him eschew evil, and do good; let him seek peace, and ensue it. (1 Peter 3:10-11)

But godliness with contentment is great gain. For we brought nothing into this world, and it is certain we can carry nothing out. And having food and raiment let us be therewith content. (1 Timothy 6:6-8)

For which of you, intending to build a tower, sitteth not down first, and counteth the cost, whether he have sufficient to finish it? Lest haply, after he hath laid the foundation, and is not able to finish it, all that behold it begin to mock him. (Luke 14:28-29)

WALK IN TRUTH

Chapter VI

WALK IN TRUTH

It is important for every believer to know he or she is responsible for walking in truth. The truth is in the Bible. We should not be conformed to this world but be transformed by the renewing of our minds. We should also prove that which is good, and acceptable, and the perfect will of God. (Romans 12:2) Believers are also responsible for living holy. We should present our bodies as a living sacrifice, holy, and acceptable unto God, which is our reasonable service according to Romans 12:1. God wants us to be holy for He is holy. This is a commandment from God found in Leviticus 11:44.

Walking with God and walking in truth requires humbleness, a teachable spirit, understanding, patience, and courage. These are some ingredients that help develop our relationship with God. As He continues to develop us we can confidently walk with Him.

We need to be humble before God. According to 1Peter 5:5 we should clothe ourselves with humility because God resisteth the proud but giveth grace to the humble. Humble means not proud or arrogant according to The Random House College Dictionary. When we are humble before an Almighty God, we are showing God that we need Him. Without Him we cannot do anything. When we are humble we can repent for our sins and get the forgiveness from God that we need.

A teachable spirit is the next thing God requires of us. When we have a teachable spirit it is admitting to God, ourselves and others that we do not know everything. We must become as little children and humble ourselves according to Matthew 18:3-4. It then allows God to use others and circumstances to teach us. God blesses us when we receive what He has for us through circumstances and other people. God wants to give us everything we need. We have to be open to receive no matter how He gets it to us.

A teachable spirit then allows us to get the right understanding about our situations. God does not want us to jump to conclusions on any situation. According to Proverbs 3:5-6, we should not lean to our understanding. God wants us to trust Him completely with our hearts so we can understand each situation in our lives. He wants us to ask Him and acknowledge Him on which direction we should take.

God then requires patience because He has a specific timing for everything. He does not want us to do anything in haste. God is at work in us and He surely is working on us. God knows what each circumstance, each situation, each failure, and each success will bring in our lives. He knows what result He is planning to get out of our lives. Remember that He has a plan and a destiny for us. He also has an architectural layout for our destiny. To accomplish it we must go under construction. Construction on anything that has a beautiful end takes time to accomplish it. It will not happen overnight. This is why we need patience.

When God finally brings us into our destiny after construction we will need courage. For God hath not given us the spirit of fear, but of power, and of love, and of a sound mind. (2 Timothy 1:7) In order to carry out the assignment God gave us, we will need tenacity, strength, holy boldness, and the audacity to do it.

When we arrive in our DESTINY we must continue to walk in truth. We must do this before God, before our family, our church, at work and in our communities. Walking consistently in truth produces integrity, respect, love, good character, favor and ultimately you will have a good name. According to Proverbs 22:1 "A good name is rather to be chosen than great riches, and loving favour rather than silver and gold."

It is our obligation to walk in truth before God because he purchased us with a price. (1 Corinthians 6:20) We belong to Him and we are the sheep of His pasture. (Psalms 100:3) We must reverence and glorify Him. He is Jehovah Jireh our provider. He is Jehovah Shalom the prince of peace. He is also Jehovah Rapha our healer. He is whatever we need Him to be. We should have no other gods before HIM. When we sin we must also be willing to confess and repent. (1 John 1:9) We should not play with God. When we worship we must worship Him in spirit and truth. (John 4:24) We cannot stand in His holy place unless we have clean hands and a pure heart according to Psalms 24:3-4. As we walk truthfully before God we must walk in truth in our homes. This means to be faithful in our marriages. It is our responsibility to keep our marriage vows to God and our spouse. The husband and wife must truly know their roles and function correctly in them. Ephesians 5:22-23 says "Wives, submit yourselves unto your own husbands, as unto the Lord. For the husband is the head of the wife, even as Christ is the head of the church: and he is the saviour of the body." For husbands Ephesians 5:25-26 says "Husbands, love your wives, even as Christ also loved the church, and gave himself for it; that he might sanctify and cleanse it with the washing of water by the word" God has set a plan for the family. When husband and wife are obedient to God's plan there will be harmony in the home.

As we rear our children we are responsible for leading them in the right way. Proverbs 22:6 says "Train up a child in the way he should go: and when he is old, he will not depart from it." Children must understand their role in the family so they will learn to be obedient. Ephesians 6:1-3 says "Children, obey your parents in the Lord: for this is right. Honour thy father and mother; which is the first commandment with promise; that it may be well with thee, and thou mayest live long on the earth." We must give our children the right tools for life. These tools are in the word of God. These principles we teach our children will give them wisdom and help them in life.

We must walk in truth in our church affiliations. We do this by obeying the by laws and rules of the church. If we serve in any office we should be good stewards. Just as Paul told Timothy in 1 Timothy 4:16 to "Take heed unto thyself, and unto the doctrine; continue in them: for in doing this thou shalt both save thyself, and them that hear thee." We should also take heed to ensure that we are walking in truth before the church.

We should walk in truth daily and not just on Sunday. During the week it is important that we walk in truth on our jobs. We should remember we work with Christians and non-Christians. It is important for our co-workers and our bosses to see Christ in us. We show Christ in our attitudes, our work habits, what we say and what we do. We should stand out as an example to others. Ephesians 6:5-9 explains how employees should work as unto the Lord and be obedient to their employers. It also explains how employers should treat their employees and not threaten them.

Our community is also important as we continue to walk in truth. We need to be mindful when we are out in public. Our actions and what we say should be in line with God's word. We should deal honestly in every business transaction. Whether we are doing business at the grocery store, bank, or department store we need to have integrity. We must make a difference in our communities at the voting poll, in community organizations, and with the kids in our community. It is our responsibility to care about what happens in our communities and stand up for what is right. We should also love one another. If we do this we are showing the world and our communities that we belong to Christ. (John 13:35)

People who walk consistently in truth will say what they mean and mean what they say. Their word will be their bond. Their walk will line up with their talk. Jesus is an excellent example. He preached and walked according to God's word. God anointed Him with the Holy Ghost and with power, and He went about doing good and healing all who were oppressed of the devil; for God was with Him. (Acts 10:38) When you are walking in holiness and truth God will be with you.

To walk in the truth and holiness consistently you must study the Bible. You must study to show thyself approved unto God, a workman that needeth not to be ashamed, rightly dividing the word of truth. (2 Timothy 2:15)

According to Ephesians 4:14, you will no longer be as children tossed to and fro, and carried about with every wind of doctrine, by the sleight of men, and cunning craftiness, whereby they lie in wait to deceive. The word of God will equip you to do what Jesus did in the wilderness after fasting. He refuted every untruth the devil tried to tell him. (Matthew 4)

Walking in truth also involves being led by the Holy Spirit. According to John 16:13 the Holy Spirit will guide you into all truth.

Truth helps us see and judge a situation for what it really is. We must also get the facts to make sure we are making the right judgment in the situation. Many times we want to believe something different from what is truly happening. When we accept the truth about a situation, we can then handle it how God wants us to. If we are personally involved in the situation we must trace all the steps to how we became involved. We need to judge ourselves truthfully and be honest about where we went wrong. In doing this we begin the healing process and open the door to allow God to deal with us truthfully. According to John 8:32, it is the truth that makes us free.

When you are consistently walking in truth and living holy God will be pleased with you. Psalms 1 lets us know that God will be pleased with the man whose delight is in the law of the Lord and who meditates day and night in His law.

It is imperative that we stop compromising the truth and walk in it. Compromising the truth keeps us off course. It keeps us from our destiny. It keeps us unfocused and it keeps us walking in a lie instead of walking in the truth. Many continue to live a life of compromise for years and years in certain areas to please family, friends, people or themselves. Sometimes we do this knowingly and other times unknowingly. In either case it displeases God and is against His word. Sometimes compromise can happen by default. Some are manipulated or tricked into compromising God's principles. Whatever the case may be, it is time to identify where you have been compromising and correct it with God.

When we correct where we have been compromising we can get back on track and continue to walk with God. If we continue doing things we know are right, we will end up in the destiny God has for us. We must also be careful of how we are building our lives. We must remember unless the Lord builds the house we are laboring in vain according to Psalms 127:1.

When we learn to discipline ourselves to walk in truth we begin to deal with God, ourselves and others in a truthful manner. We deal honestly in our personal and business affairs. We also become spiritually mature. We must consistently measure ourselves against the word of God to see if we are meeting or missing the mark. We must keep in mind that Christ is the standard. The word of God is the absolute truth by which we need to live our lives.

Now that we have been taught not to compromise and to walk in truth before God, in our homes, in our church, on the job and in our community we must now be placed on trial. The question now is CAN YOU PASS THE TEST?

Personal Testimony..................

God has delivered me from compromising his word and feeling obligated to please people. When you live a life of compromise you are not walking in truth. We should never feel obligated to compromise God's word to please people.

Prayer......................

Heavenly Father thank you for giving the world in the beginning the absolute truth through creation, through men of God you chose, and through your word.

Thank you for the Holy Bible so I can have a standard by which to live my life. A standard that will remain the same no matter what era of life it is. Thank you for growing me to a point of maturity to line things up against the word of God.

Thank you that I no longer have to be deceived or tricked by the philosophies of men that are contrary to your word. Help me to walk in truth in private and public. Help me to put off all masks and phony personalities that hide my real self. Help me to love myself for who I am and to be who you called me to be.

Help me to be truthful in my relationship with you, my neighbor, and with myself. Help me to speak the truth, walk in truth, and be accountable to the standard of truth. Remind me when I make a mistake and error away from the truth to correct it as soon as possible. In Jesus Name, Amen.

Brenda Diann Johnson

Further Study.....

If we say that we have no sin, we deceive ourselves, and the truth is not in us. (1 John 1:8)

Sanctify them through thy truth: thy word is truth. (John 17:17)

For what if some did not believe? Shall their unbelief make the faith of God without effect? God forbid: yea, let God be true, but every man a liar; as it is written, That thou mightest be justified in thy sayings, and mightest overcome when thou art judged. (Romans 3:3-4)

God is not a man, that he should lie, neither the son of man, that he should repent: hath he said, and shall he not do it? Or hath he spoken, and shall he not make it good? (Numbers 23:19)

That we henceforth be no more children, tossed to and fro, and carried about with every wind of doctrine, by the sleight of men, and cunning craftiness, whereby they lie in wait to deceive; But speaking the truth in love, may grow up into him in all things, which is the head, even Christ. (Ephesians 4:14-15)

For men shall be lovers of their own selves, covetous, boasters, proud, blasphemers, disobedient to parents, unthankful, unholy, without natural affection, trucebreakers, false accusers, incontinent, fierce, despisers of those that are good, traitors, heady, highminded, lovers of pleasure more than lovers of God; Having a form of godliness, but denying the power thereof: from such turn away. (2 Timothy 3:2-5)

Now the works of the flesh are manifest, which are these; Adultery, fornication, uncleanness, lasciviousness, idolatry, witchcraft, hatred, variance, emulations, wrath, strife, seditions, heresies, envyings, murders, drunkenness, revellings, and such like: of the which I tell you before, as I have also told you in time past, that they which do such things shall not inherit the kingdom of God. (Galatians 5:19-21)

Howbeit when he, the Spirit of truth, is come, he will guide you into all truth: for he shall not speak of himself; but whatsoever he shall hear, that shall he speak: and he will shew you things to come. (John 16:13)

And even as they did not like to retain God in their knowledge, God gave them over to a reprobate mind, to do those things which are not convenient. (Romans 1:28)

Now the Spirit speaketh expressly, that in the latter times some shall depart from the faith, giving heed to seducing spirits, and doctrines of devils; Speaking lies in hypocrisy; having their conscience seared with a hot iron; Forbidding to marry, and commanding to abstain from meats, which God hath created to be received with thanksgiving of them which believe and know the truth. (1Timothy 4:1-3)

They are of the world: therefore speak they of the world, and the world heareth them. We are of God: he that knoweth God heareth us; he that is not of God heareth not us. Hereby know we the spirit of truth, and the spirit of error. (1 John 4:5-6)

Then said Jesus to those Jews which believed on him, If ye continue in my word, then are ye my disciples indeed; And ye shall know the truth, and the truth shall make you free. (John 8:31-32)

Who shall ascend into the hill of the Lord? Or who shall stand in his holy place? He that hath clean hands, and a pure heart; who hath not lifted up his soul unto vanity, nor sworn deceitfully. (Psalms 24:3-4)

CAN YOU PASS THE TEST?

Chapter VII

CAN YOU PASS THE TEST?

As we continue to walk in truth throughout life, we will have trials and tribulations. These are tests or divine appointments from God. There will also be times of tribulations that the enemy has placed on us. God wants to build our faith. The enemy wants to attack and destroy our faith. God wants us to grow in certain areas. The enemy wants to tear down and sift us as wheat and cause us to give up. When we encounter these trials and tribulations they are only for a certain period or season. God's testing strategically brings the best result for our lives. When the enemy puts something on us, it is to attack and destroy what God is trying to build in us. There are many tests God designed for each of us. He knows what we need individually. In either case we will encounter the FAITH TEST, the DELAY TEST, and the BELIEF TEST.

When we encounter the FAITH TEST God is at work in us. Faith is the substance of things hoped for and the evidence of things not seen. (Hebrews 11:1) According to the Random House College Dictionary, Faith is confidence or trust in a person or thing. It is belief not based on proof.

We must first and foremost trust that God is teaching us something. We must trust that He is the teacher and we are the students. No matter how bad things look we must trust that God has a purpose in this trial of FAITH to teach us something.

Brenda Diann Johnson

Sometimes when we find ourselves in this particular kind of test we don't understand at first what is happening. We don't know what God is doing in our lives. He could be working on our character to add or cut something away from us. Whatever God is doing we need to trust that it is for our own good. It is to make us a better person and to conform us to Christ's image.

God wants to bring out the best in us. This is why we should count it all joy when we fall into divers temptations; knowing this, that the trying of our faith worketh patience. But let patience have her perfect work, that we may be perfect and entire, wanting nothing. (James 1:2-4) Another word for patience is endurance. God wants to help us endure through our various trials.

Sometimes God sends trials and tribulations to produce a certain type of fruit in us where we need it. Another way of looking at fruit is God produces a certain character trait in us that we need. The fruits of the Spirit are love, joy, peace, long-suffering, gentleness, goodness, faith, meekness, and temperance according to Galatians 5:22-23. After we grow and develop these fruits of the spirit we become mature in handling the issues of life.

The next test that we may encounter is the DELAY TEST. According to the Random House College Dictionary, Delay means to put off to a later time. To defer, postpone, to impede the progress of; retard or hinder.

This test can either be from God or the enemy. When the enemy is at work he orchestrates this test. The enemy's purpose is that of an antagonist. He wants to frustrate, delay and ultimately destroy God's plan for our lives. The enemy wants to delay whenever he gets an open opportunity to do so. We also go through trials of delay because of decisions we have made. Some of our trials come as a result of our own temptations that we deal with. These temptations that we allow to overtake us can cause a delay to our destiny.

These temptations we have can get us into a lot of trouble or kill us. The death could be spiritual or physical. We encounter these trials because of our own temptations according to James 1:13-15. "Let no man say when he is tempted, I am being tempted of God: for God cannot be tempted with evil, neither tempteth he any man: But every man is tempted, when he is drawn away of his own lust, and enticed. Then when lust hath conceived, it bringeth forth sin: and sin, when it is finished, bringeth forth death."

Many times we are tempted by the very thing we like or desire strongly in our hearts. As Christians we should make sure that our desires line up with God's desire for us. God wants us to have the best and He knows what we need and what we want. He wants to send these desires, needs, and wants to us through His way of doing things. He does not want us to sin to get what we need, want, or desire. When we know where the enemy is tricking us, we should lay aside every weight and the sin which doth so easily beset us, and let us run with patience the race that is set before us. (Hebrews 12:1)

We are delayed when we are given wrong information intentionally and unintentionally. Satan uses people to lead us in the wrong direction and to plot our demise. Just like God knows what we want, our adversary the devil also knows. Remember his mission is to kill, steal, and destroy. Our adversary the devil, as a roaring lion, walketh about, seeking whom he may devour according to 1 Peter 5:8.

Many times we are tricked by the adversary. He shows us something we desire and he makes it look like a blessing from God. When the adversary brings you something, you have to sin to get it. The adversary will have you doing something out of your character. He will have you lying, cheating, stealing, or deceiving to get what you want or need. If you have to do something wrong that should be a red flag to you. You should know that what you are about to receive is not from God. God will not have you doing anything against the principles He has set in His word.

The DELAY TEST can also be sent to us by God. God wants us to receive all that He has for us. There is a right and a wrong way for us to get what He has for us. In James 1:16-17 it says "Do not err, my beloved brethren. Every good gift and every perfect gift is from above, and cometh down from the Father of lights, with whom is no variableness, neither shadow of turning."

God knows life will bring us the tests and trials He sends and those the adversary sends our way. Even when the adversary sets traps for us, God allows it for a reason. Even when we fall into the devil's trap, God is still there to work it out. According to 1 Corinthians 10:13-14, it says "There hath no temptation taken you but such as is common to man: but God is faithful, who will not suffer you to be tempted above that ye are able; but will with the temptation also make a way to escape, that ye may be able to bear it. Wherefore, my dearly beloved, flee from idolatry."

We are also delayed by circumstances that don't discriminate. These are unfortunate things that can happen to anyone at anytime. It could be a matter of geographical location, economics, environment, or weather. As we go through life and encounter trials we must remember that others encounter trials and tribulations as well. No one in life is exempt from having good and bad times, ups and downs, sadness and happiness. These come with the issues of life. We must be also willing to help others endure through their trials and tribulations. We must comfort others just like God comforted us and brought people to help us, according to 2 Corinthians 1: 3-4.

During the times we are delayed through trials and tribulations, our own disobedience, or a trap from Satan, we should humble ourselves. According to 1 Peter 5:6-7, we are to humble ourselves therefore under the mighty hand of God, that He may exalt us in due time. Casting all our cares upon him; for he careth for us. Whatever the purpose God has for the trial, we should ask Him to help and instruct us through it. We should also seek an understanding from God for the trial according to Proverbs 3:5-6. We must trust in the Lord with all our heart and lean not unto our own understanding. In all our ways we should acknowledge Him and He shall direct our paths. When we seek God's understanding for the trial we will learn the lesson in it.

Many times people become frustrated when they are delayed. They get angry when they can't make progress in their lives. They feel God's principles are too hard so they create their own method to achieve their goals. Many create their own way even if it is wrong, illegal, and ungodly. They also create methods without boundaries and constraints. Anything goes when the absolute standard has been forsaken. Instead of seeking God for help to obey His principles they become upset and frustrated with God. God's principles require discipline and obedience. Many times people are unwilling to give what it takes to be disciplined or obedient. The more we become disciplined in a specific area of our lives the easier it will become to be obedient in that same area.

God will only support, hold together, defend, and bless His principles and His word. He is not obligated to bless something that we have come up with. If we follow God's principles and learn the lessons that He takes us through we will grow. We will become the person God wants us to be and He will bless us. He will not withhold any good thing from us when we walk uprightly according to Psalms 84:11. Many times we choose another way because we feel God is withholding something we want. We get angry and impatient and abandon the process God is taking us through. We create and manipulate a way to get what we want. God would gladly give us what we want but with discipline and obedience.

God will supply all our needs according to His riches in glory by Christ Jesus. (Philippians 4:19) The blessings God has prepared for us requires discipline and obedience. He wants us to be prepared for the blessings that He has for us so we will be good stewards. According to 3 John 1:2, it is imperative that we also prosper in our souls. God wants to bless us in our health, soul and those material blessing that we need in the world.

We must also watch how we live and the things we teach other people. We must watch what we say and do, even how we live our lives. We must be an example or ambassador for Christ. In watching how we live our lives this will save us and those that we teach. This was the same instruction that Paul gave Timothy in 1Timothy 4:16. We must allow God to direct and guide us to the DESTINY He originally ordained for us. We must allow Him to build our lives, our career, our family, and our businesses. If we don't let God build what concerns us then we are laboring in vain according to Psalms 127:1.

Sometimes we have flaws and dysfunctions that God has addressed for years. Instead of correcting the dysfunction

Brenda Diann Johnson

many times we find someone or a crowd of people to match, encourage, accept or approve of our dysfunction. Never looking inside ourselves and asking God to help change us to line up with His word. Instead we start hanging with the wrong crowd. Not realizing that evil communications corrupt good manners according to 1 Corinthians 15:33. All of us have issues and dysfunctions. Hanging with the wrong crowd will make things worse. We should hang around the right people who are following God's word. They will help us to correct our dysfunction and encourage us to do what is right.

There are practical things that can be done in our lives that will solve some of the problems we have. Those things outside us can be solved practically and are at our disposal to work out. Those things inside us are what God works on. He takes us through trials and tribulations to produce fruit inside us. This helps us to grow and mature on the inside so that we can deal effectively with our problems on the outside. This helps us to deal better with life issues as we encounter them. We can now do this successfully because of the maturity or fruit that we have bore on the inside.

As we continue to grow and walk in the way of truth we will encounter the BELIEF TEST. Belief according to the Random House College Dictionary means to have confidence in the truth or existence of something not immediately susceptible to rigorous proof.

The adversary will get more aggressive as we grow and

get victory over many situations in our lives. When we are tried by the enemy, he will try everything he can until he fails. Even though he fails he will leave us for awhile and come back later in a different form. This test is designed to see if we have a form of godliness but have denied the power thereof. (2 Timothy 3:5) An example of this is when the enemy came on the scene in Matthew 4 to put Jesus on trial. The enemy tried Jesus' belief in the word of God. The enemy challenged Jesus' knowledge of the word of God. The enemy will always do this aggressively. This is why we must KNOW in whom and what we believe.

He wants to confuse you about your knowledge of the word of God. This is why we should not look at, listen to, walk in, or entertain a lie. Proverbs 4:14-15 says enter not into the path of the wicked, and go not in the way of evil men. Avoid it, pass not by it, turn from it, and pass away. If we make the mistake of listening to the enemy and entertain him, he can get a foot in the door. Once he gets us to listen to what he says, he will persuade us to believe him. If we believe him, he can get us to do and say things that are not of God. This will then damage our character, integrity, our ministry, the way we live, and our faith in God.

The enemy also comes when we are going through a trial that God is taking us through. Many times we are tempted to listen or consider the way of the wicked when we are going through trials and tribulations. We get impatient and we see the wicked seemingly doing well. David almost made this mistake according to Psalm 73:2-3. David said "But as for me, my feet were almost gone; my steps had well nigh slipped. For I was envious at the foolish, when I saw the prosperity of the wicked."

In Psalm 73 David was discouraged about his situation until he entered God's sanctuary. He was able to hear the truth about the destiny of the wicked. We forget about God's promises to us when we look at the prosperity of the wicked. We need to keep our minds, our eyes, our ears, our heart and soul stayed on God. God knows what we have need of. He is concerned about the pain and suffering we are going through.

We should not be ignorant of Satan's devices, lest he should get an advantage over of us. (2 Corinthians 2:11) When we are going through our trials and tribulations the enemy wants to paint a picture that God has forgotten about us. The enemy wants us to believe that God does not care and somehow is not able to deliver us. The enemy does this to entice us to come over to his side. The adversary wants us to give up on God and His will for our lives. The enemy wants us to try another way contrary to what God has told us. If we continue to look and listen long enough we will find ourselves going in the way of the wicked. Before the devil's plan begins to take root, we need to stand firm and give no opportunity to the enemy.

In those times of despair God will always send encouragement and hope to us through someone. He will place worthy people in our lives to help us pass the test. They will minister to us and not allow us to fall. They will help us in practical and biblical ways. They will minister to us when we are hurting and sad. They will help clarify our questions about the word of God. They will challenge us and help us grow. They will also love us unconditionally and are willing to share similar experiences from their lives to help us. These are God's ambassadors who are sent to minister to the saints. They are led by the Holy Spirit and are ready for service no matter where God may lead.

Personal Testimony.................

I used my faith when I was laid off my job. I had faith that God would take care of my daughter and me. He took care of us. We did not go one day without eating or the bills being paid. God honored my faith in Him.

Prayer......................

Dear Heavenly Father I want to thank you for giving your children the victory before hand. Thank you that the race is fixed and our destiny is secure. Thank you that I have been predestined and justified by you.

Help me Father to stand strong in faith and not waver on the convictions of what I believe in your word. Even when I am delayed help me to be steadfast and unmovable and always abounding in your word. Keep me from being discouraged so easily when trouble comes. Help me to hold fast to my confession. Help me to keep my tongue from speaking death and only to speak life in times of trouble.

Help me to walk by faith and not by sight. Help me to remember that no matter how bad things get you are still in control. Help me to learn the lessons you have for me in every trial and tribulation. Continue to be my shelter, my strength, my provider, my protector and my encourager in uncertain times. Because I trust in you I can confidently say like Job "When I have been tried, I will come forth as pure gold" In Jesus Name, Amen.

Further Study

Faith Test.........

Now faith is the substance of things hoped for, the evidence of things not seen. (Hebrews 11:1)

But without faith it is impossible to please him: for he that cometh to God must believe that he is, and that he is a rewarder of them that diligently seek him. (Hebrews 11:6)

For by grace are ye saved through faith; and that not of yourselves: it is the gift of God. (Ephesians 2:8)

But before faith came, we were kept under the law, shut up unto the faith which should afterwards be revealed.

Wherefore the law was our schoolmaster to bring us unto Christ, that we might be justified by faith. But after that faith is come, we are no longer under a schoolmaster. For ye are all the children of God by faith in Christ Jesus. (Galatians 3:23-26)

But the fruit of the Spirit is love, joy, peace, longsuffering, gentleness, goodness, faith, meekness, temperance: against such there is no law. (Galatians 5:22-23)

I am crucified with Christ: nevertheless I live; yet not I, but Christ liveth in me: and the life which I now live in the flesh I live by the faith of the Son of God, who loved me, and gave himself for me. (Galatians 2:20)

For we walk by faith, not by sight. (2 Corinthians 5:7)

And Jesus answering saith unto them, Have faith in God. For verily I say unto you, that whosoever shall say unto this mountain, Be thou removed, and be thou cast into the sea; and shall not doubt in his heart, but shall believe that those things which he saith shall come to pass; he shall have whatsoever he saith. (Mark 11:22-23)

If we believe not, yet he abideth faithful: he cannot deny himself. (2 Timothy 2:13)

For whatsoever is born of God overcometh the world: and this is the victory that overcometh the world, even our faith. (1 John 5:4)

But the Lord is faithful, who shall stablish you, and keep you from evil. (2 Thessalonians 3:3)

These things I have spoken unto you, that in me ye might have peace. In the world ye shall have tribulation: but be of good cheer; I have overcome the world. (John 16:33)

Be of good courage, and he shall strengthen your heart, all ye that hope in the Lord. (Psalms 31:24)

For thou art my hope, O Lord God: thou art my trust from my youth. (Psalms 71:5)

Who by him do believe in God, that raised him up from the dead, and gave him glory; that your faith and hope might be in God. (1 Peter 1:21)

Why art thou cast down, O my soul? and why art thou disquieted within me? hope thou in God: for I shall yet praise him, who is the health of my countenance, and my God. (Psalms 42:11)

Delay Test.......

Wherefore seeing we also are compassed about with so great a cloud of witnesses, let us lay aside every weight, and the sin which doth so easily beset us, and let us run with patience the race that is set before us. (Hebrews 12:1)

For a just man falleth seven times, and riseth up again: but the wicked shall fall into mischief. (Proverbs 24:16)

Now the just shall live by faith: but if any man draw back, my soul shall have no pleasure in him. But we are not of them who draw back unto perdition; but of them that believe to the saving of the soul. (Hebrews 10:38-39)

A merry heart doeth good like a medicine: but a broken spirit drieth the bones. (Proverbs 17:22)

All the days of the afflicted are evil: but he that is of a merry heart hath a continual feast. (Proverbs 15:15)

For what glory is it, if when ye be buffeted for your faults, ye shall take it patiently? but if, when ye do well, and suffer for it, ye take it patiently, this is acceptable with God. (1 Peter 2:20)

And let us not be weary in well doing: for in due season we shall reap, if we faint not. (Galatians 6:9)

But he that shall endure unto the end, the same shall be saved. (Matthew 24:13)

And we desire that every one of you do shew the same diligence to the full assurance of hope unto the end: That ye be not slothful, but followers of them who through faith and patience inherit the promises. (Hebrews 6:11-12)

For ye have need of patience, that, after ye have done the will of God, ye might receive the promise. (Hebrews 10:36)

Brenda Diann Johnson

My brethren, count it all joy when ye fall into divers temptations; Knowing this, that the trying of your faith worketh patience. But let patience have her perfect work, that ye may be perfect and entire, wanting nothing. (James 1:2-4)

And not only so, but we glory in tribulations also: knowing that tribulation worketh patience; and patience, experience, and experience, hope: and hope maketh not ashamed; because the love of God is shed abroad in our hearts by the Holy Ghost which is given unto us. (Romans 5:3-5)

Many are the afflictions of the righteous: but the Lord delivereth him out of them all. (Psalms 34:19)

Yea, and all that will live godly in Christ Jesus shall suffer persecution. (2 Timothy 3:12)

Thou therefore endure hardness, as a good soldier of Jesus Christ. (2 Timothy 2:3)

Preach the word; be instant in season, out of season; reprove, rebuke, exhort with all longsuffering and doctrine. (2 Timothy 4:2)

My brethren, count it all joy when ye fall into divers temptations; knowing this, that the trying of your faith worketh patience. But let patience have her perfect work, that ye may be perfect and entire, wanting nothing. (James 1:2-4)

Beloved, think it not strange concerning the fiery trial which is to try you, as though some strange thing happened unto you: But rejoice, inasmuch as ye are partakers of Christ's sufferings; that, when his glory shall be revealed, ye may be glad also with exceeding joy. (1 Peter 4:12-13)

For I am persuaded, that neither death, nor life, nor angels, nor principalities, nor powers, nor things present, nor things to come, Nor height, nor depth, nor any other creature, shall be able to separate us from the love of God, which is in Christ Jesus our Lord. (Romans 8:38-39)

My Father, which gave them me, is greater than all; and no man is able to pluck them out of my Father's hand. I and my Father are one. (John 10:29-30)

Be still, and know that I am God: I will be exalted among the heathen, I will be exalted in the earth. (Psalms 46:10)

Lord, they have killed thy prophets, and digged down thine altars; and I am left alone, and they seek my life. But what saith the answer of God unto him? I have reserved to myself seven thousand men, who have not bowed the knee to the image of Baal. (Romans 11:3-4)

For a great door and effectual is opened unto me, and there are many adversaries. (1 Corinthians 16:9)

Belief Test.......

Jesus said unto him, If thou canst believe, all things are possible to him that believeth. And straightway the father of the child cried out, and said with tears, Lord, I believe; help thou mine unbelief. (Mark 9:23-24)

For the which cause I also suffer these things: nevertheless I am not ashamed: for I know whom I have believed, and am persuaded that he is able to keep that which I have committed unto him against that day. (2 Timothy 1:12)

For God so loved the world, that he gave his only begotten Son, that whosoever believeth in him should not perish, but have everlasting life. (John 3:16)

He that believeth on the Son hath everlasting life: and he that believeth not the Son shall not see life; but the wrath of God abideth on him. (John 3:36)

And they said, Believe on the Lord Jesus Christ, and thou shalt be saved, and thy house. (Acts 16:31)

And Jesus said unto them, I am the bread of life: he that cometh to me shall never hunger; and he that believeth on me shall never thirst. (John 6:35)

Jesus saith unto him, Thomas, because thou hast seen me, thou hast believed: blessed are they that have not seen, and yet have believed. (John 20:29)

Behold, I give unto you power to tread on serpents and scorpions, and over all the power of the enemy: and nothing shall by any means hurt you. (Luke 10:19)

And I say also unto thee, That thou art Peter, and upon this rock I will build my church; and the gates of hell shall not prevail against it. (Matthew 16:18)

And I will give unto thee the keys of the kingdom of heaven: and whatsoever thou shalt bind on earth shall be bound in heaven: and whatsoever thou shalt loose on earth shall be loosed in heaven (Matthew 16:19)

For God hath not given us the spirit of fear, but of power, and of love, and of a sound mind. (2 Timothy 1:7)

For with God nothing shall be impossible. (Luke 1:37)

Surely he shall deliver thee from the snare of the fowler, and from the noisome pestilence. (Psalms 91:3)

Though I walk in the midst of trouble, thou wilt revive me: thou shalt stretch forth thine hand against the wrath of mine enemies, and thy right hand shall save me. The Lord will perfect that which concerneth me: thy mercy, O Lord, endureth for ever: forsake not the works of thine own hands. (Psalms 138:7-8)

Notwithstanding the Lord stood with me, and strengthened me; that by me the preaching might be fully known, and that all the Gentiles might hear: and I was delivered out of the mouth of the lion. And the Lord shall deliver me from every evil work, and will preserve me unto his heavenly kingdom: to whom be glory forever and ever. Amen. (2 Timothy 4:17-18)

The Lord is my rock, and my fortress, and my deliverer; my God, my strength, in whom I will trust; my buckler, and the horn of my salvation, and my high tower. I will call upon the Lord, who is worthy to be praised: so shall I be saved from mine enemies. (Psalms 18:2-3)

I Shall not die, but live, and declare the works of the Lord. (Psalm 118:17)

No weapon that is formed against thee shall prosper; and every tongue that shall rise against thee in judgment thou shalt condemn. This is the heritage of the servants of the Lord, and their righteousness is of me, saith the Lord. (Isaiah 54:17)

If ye abide in me, and my words abide in you, ye shall ask what ye will, and it shall be done unto you. (John 15:7)

Verily, verily, I say unto you, He that believeth on me, the works that I do shall he do also; and greater works than these shall he do; because I go unto my Father. And whatsoever ye shall ask in my name, that will I do, that the Father may be glorified in the Son. If ye shall ask any thing in my name, I will do it. (John 14:12-14)

God is not a man, that he should lie, neither the son of man, that he should repent: hath he said, and shall he not do it? Or hath he spoken, and shall he not make it good? (Numbers 23:19)

CONCLUSION

CONCLUSION

In conclusion, life will be full of victories, defeats, and challenges. I am confident that you and I will overcome all adversities. We must not be weary in well doing: for in due season we shall reap, if we faint not. (Galatians 6:9) There will be seasons of planting, plucking up, building, tearing down, happiness, and sadness. There will be times when we feel we are all alone. Even though others may not understand what we are going through it is ok as long as God knows. People who do not understand your season may whisper and talk about you. Remember it is ok. As long as you understand your season let others stay in their confusion.

According to Ecclesiastes 3, to everything there is a season and a time to every purpose under the heaven. When it is your season to build, start building. When it is time for God to tear down some things in your life then submit quickly to the process. Make sure you have a clear understanding of what God wants you to do while he is at work in you. When God finishes, you can say like Job "But he knoweth the way that I take: when he hath tried me, I shall come forth as gold." (Job 23:10)

For everyone who reads this book, I want you to know that I am praying that you reach your DESTINY and be fulfilled. My prayer is also that your journey will be exciting. Make sure you take time to learn the lessons that God wants to teach you. Be encouraged when things do not turn out the way you had planned or anticipated. Remember that we are here to fulfill God's plan and not our own. It is only GOD'S WILL that will happen. Ask God to help you find your purpose in life and to help you fulfill it.

I leave you with this........You will be successful, You will overcome, You will get the victory, You are a vessel of honor, You are more than a conqueror, You are God's child and You belong to a royal family so look up and LIVE IN YOUR DESTINY!!!!

About the Author

Brenda Diann Johnson was born in Dallas, Texas on September 14, 1970 to Robert Johnson and Thelma Byrd. She is the oldest of five children. She has a brother, sister, and two half brothers.

Brenda received her education from the Dallas and Wharton, Texas school systems. She graduated from Government, Law, and Law Enforcement Magnet High School in Dallas. She also received her Bachelor of Arts degree in Communications (Broadcast News) from UTA in Arlington, Texas and her Masters of Education Degree from Strayer University. She has her Texas license in Life, Health, Accident & HMO insurance, her Texas Adjusters License in All Lines and she is a Texas Notary Public.

Today, Brenda is the CEO/Founder of The Young Scholar's Book Club which is a non-profit organization, ASWIFTT PUBLISHING, LLC which is the parent company of ASWIFTT Radio, The ASWIFTT Journal, ASWIFTT Television and ASWIFTT Records. She is an experienced educator who has taught and tutored Pre-K through College. Brenda is the Dean of Education, Curriculum & Instruction for Best Practices Training Institute. (B.P.T.I.) She has also authored books and articles.

From 2001 to 2002, Brenda served as the chairperson for an entrepreneur group called STEP (Sowing Toward Everlasting Prosperity) and as the Potter's House Center Leader for the Plan Fund.

Brenda has served as a Sunday school teacher since age 18. She has faithfully served at Tabernacle Missionary Baptist Church, Oak Cliff Bible Fellowship, Rising Star Missionary Baptist Church, and The Potter's House. She is currently a member of Prestonwood Baptist Church. In the community, Brenda has served as a volunteer to organizations that help AIDS, HIV, and Syphilis patients.

Brenda currently lives in the Dallas/Fort Worth area with her family.

Services and Books at brendadiannjohnson.com

ASWIFTT PUBLISHING, LLC

Business advertising for Print & Media

BOOK PUBLISHING

ASWIFTT RADIO

ASWIFTT T.V.

THE ASWIFTT JOURNAL Newspaper

We have affordable advertising packages in our media categories. Some Ads are as low as $35.00.

You can visit us online or e-mail us:
www.aswifttpublishing.com
aswifttbookpublishing@yahoo.com

ASWIFTT RADIO
THE ASWIFTT JOURNAL
ASWIFTT TELEVISION

(Ambassadors Sent With Information For This Time) All three (3) mediums focus on delivering timely, newsworthy and accurate news stories. They also report on local, regional, national and international topics. For more information on ASWIFTT Radio, The ASWIFTT Journal and ASWIFTT Television visit the parent company ASWIFTT Publishing.

The Young Scholar's Workbook: Book I Vol. I (www.tysbookclub.org)

The Young Scholar's Workbook: Book I Vol. I is a fundraiser publication for The Young Scholar's Book Club. 50% of the proceeds go to help keep mentoring and tutoring services free to students. $19.95 plus s/h

Advertise in an upcoming

ASWIFTT PUBLISHING, LLC Book

Your business will have a permanent advertising spot in An ASWIFTT PUBLISHING, LLC Book. The book that carries your Business Ad will continue to advertise your business every time the book is printed and purchased by a customer. For information on book advertising email us at: aswifttbookpublishing@yahoo.com

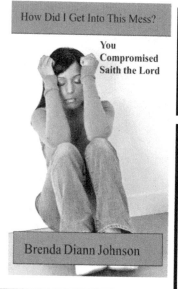

How Did I Get Into This Mess?

You Compromised Saith the Lord

Brenda Diann Johnson

$35.00 Business Ad

Includes:

1. Business Name
2. Address

$100.00 Business Ad

Includes:

1. Logo
2. Business Name
3. Address
4. Phone Number
5. Website
6. Short Bio

$65.00 Business Ad

Includes:

1. Logo
2. Business Name
3. Address
4. Phone Number
5. Website

ASWIFTT PUBLISHING, LLC ORDER FORM

Name_____

Address_____

City_____

State_____

Zip_____

Item _____Amount_____

Item _____Amount_____

Item _____Amount_____

Add $8.50 for Shipping and Handling on books

Total:_____

Make Checks, Money Orders, Cashier's Checks out to:

ASWIFTT PUBLISHING, LLC

P.O. Box 380669

Duncanville, Texas 75138

Credit Card Orders:

Circle One: Master Card   Visa   American Express Discover

Credit Card Number_____

Exp. Date_____

Three Digit Security Number on back of Card_____

Name & Address Associated with Credit Card:

_____

_____   _____

Authorization Signature　　　　**Date**

Your order will be processed or shipped 2 to 4 weeks from the date order is received. Direct concerns on orders email: aswifttbookpublishing@yahoo.com

Thank you for your business! Make copies of this form.

Made in the USA
Middletown, DE
02 June 2023

31665201R00070